I WOULDN'T LET ...
AN ELEPHANT RIDE A SKATEBOARD

By
Paul Mason

Illustrated by
Pipi Sposito

WAYLAND

First published in Great Britain in 2026
by Wayland
© Hodder and Stoughton Limited, 2026
All rights reserved

Credits:
Series Editor: Melanie Palmer
Design: Lisa Peacock
Illustrations: Pipi Sposito

ISBN hb 978 1 5263 3100 7
ISBN pb 978 1 5263 3101 4

Printed and bound in Dubai

Wayland
An imprint of
Hachette Children's Group
Part of Hodder and Stoughton Limited
Carmelite House
50 Victoria Embankment
London EC4Y 0DZ

An Hachette UK Company
www.hachette.co.uk
www.hachettechildrens.co.uk

The authorised representative in the EEA is
Hachette Ireland, 8 Castlecourt Centre,
Dublin 15, D15 XTP3, Ireland
(email: info@hbgi.ie).

CONTENTS

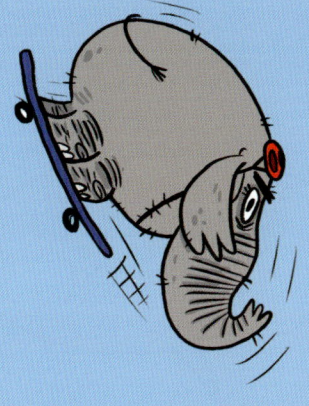

Little elephant's big surprise	4
A cracking time	6
Balance: moving and not moving	8
Rolling along	10
Speed thief (part 1)	12
Downhill all the way!	14
Learn to turn	16
Slalom skills	18
Hard stop!	20
At the skate park	22
Speed thief (part 2)	24
Faster, faster!	26
Skate school for elephants?	28
Bonus elephant facts	30
Glossary	31
Index	32

LITTLE ELEPHANT'S BIG SURPRISE

An elephant troupe is wandering through town – where its littlest member sees an amazing thing ...

"Keep up, little elephant!"

"What is THAT?"

WHOOSH!

SKATE PARK

You might think that elephants and skateboarding don't really go together ...

... you'd be wrong, though.

A CRACKING TIME

The first step to becoming the world's first skate elephant is getting a good skateboard.

Panel 1:

Well done, little elephant! There's just one problem ...

I'm not going anywhere?

CREAK! GROAN!

Panel 2:

Yes. But actually there might be another problem.

TWO problems?

CRACK!

Oh, yes, I see.

YOU'LL JUST HAVE TO GET A STRONGER SKATEBOARD DECK AND TRY AGAIN.

BALANCE: MOVING AND NOT MOVING

The skateboard deck broke because a force called weight bent it until it broke.

The skateboard broke because a strong force pushed on it. A stronger skateboard wouldn't have bent, then broken.

One like this?

Has this given you any ideas how to move the skateboard along?

Let me guess ... with a push?

PUSH

MOTION

Good work! You are right again.

ROLLING ALONG

It's time to try skateboarding again – but with a stronger, elephant-weight deck.

SPEED THIEF (PART 1)

The little elephant's skateboard started moving with a push. So what slowed it down?

The answer is a pulling force called friction.

So FRICTION pulled me back?

Exactly. Friction happens between things that are moving. For example:

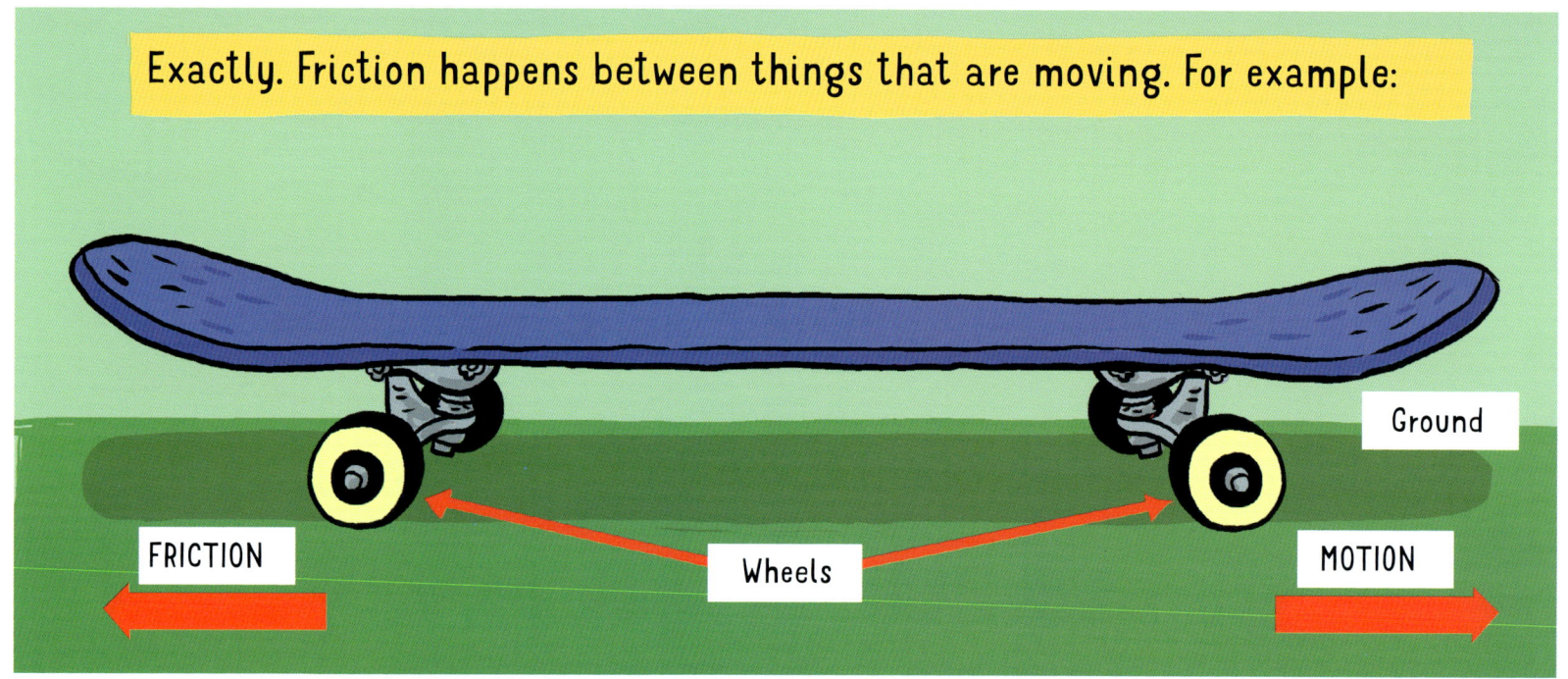

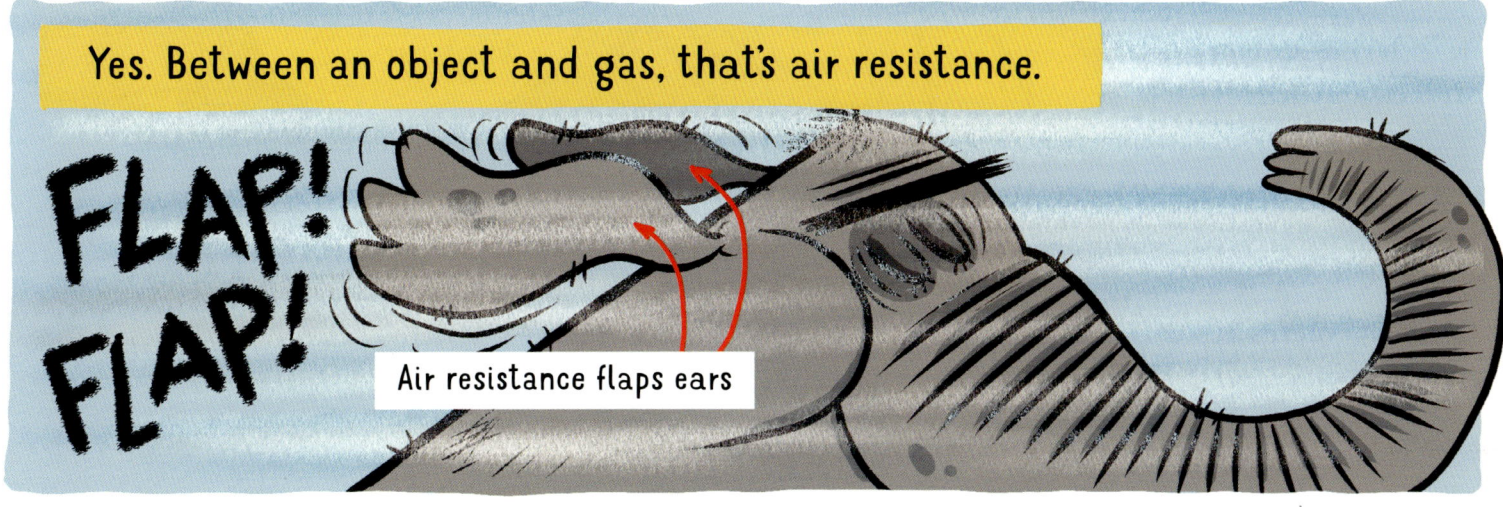

DOWNHILL ALL THE WAY!

There's another force that might make it easier to learn skateboarding – or at least go faster.

LEARN TO TURN

The skateboard went straight on because nothing made it change direction.

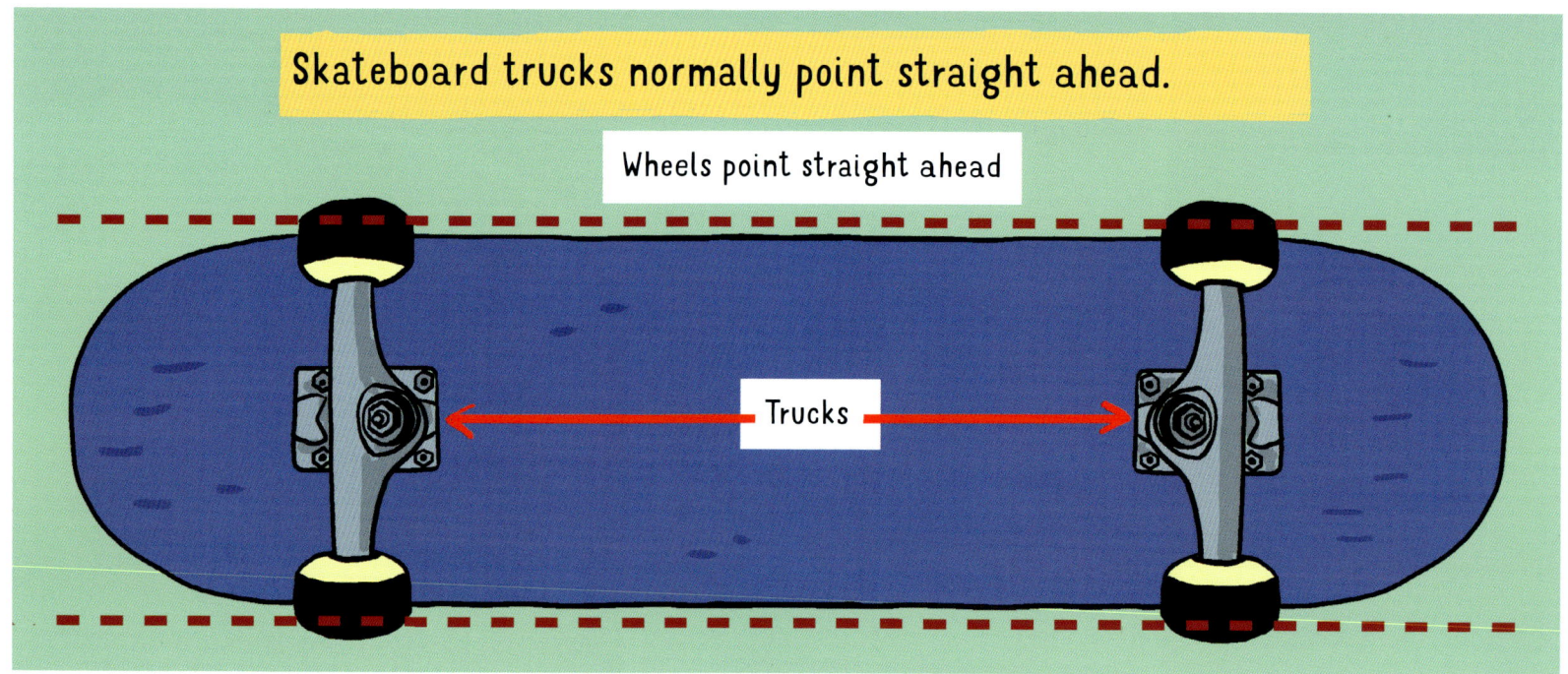

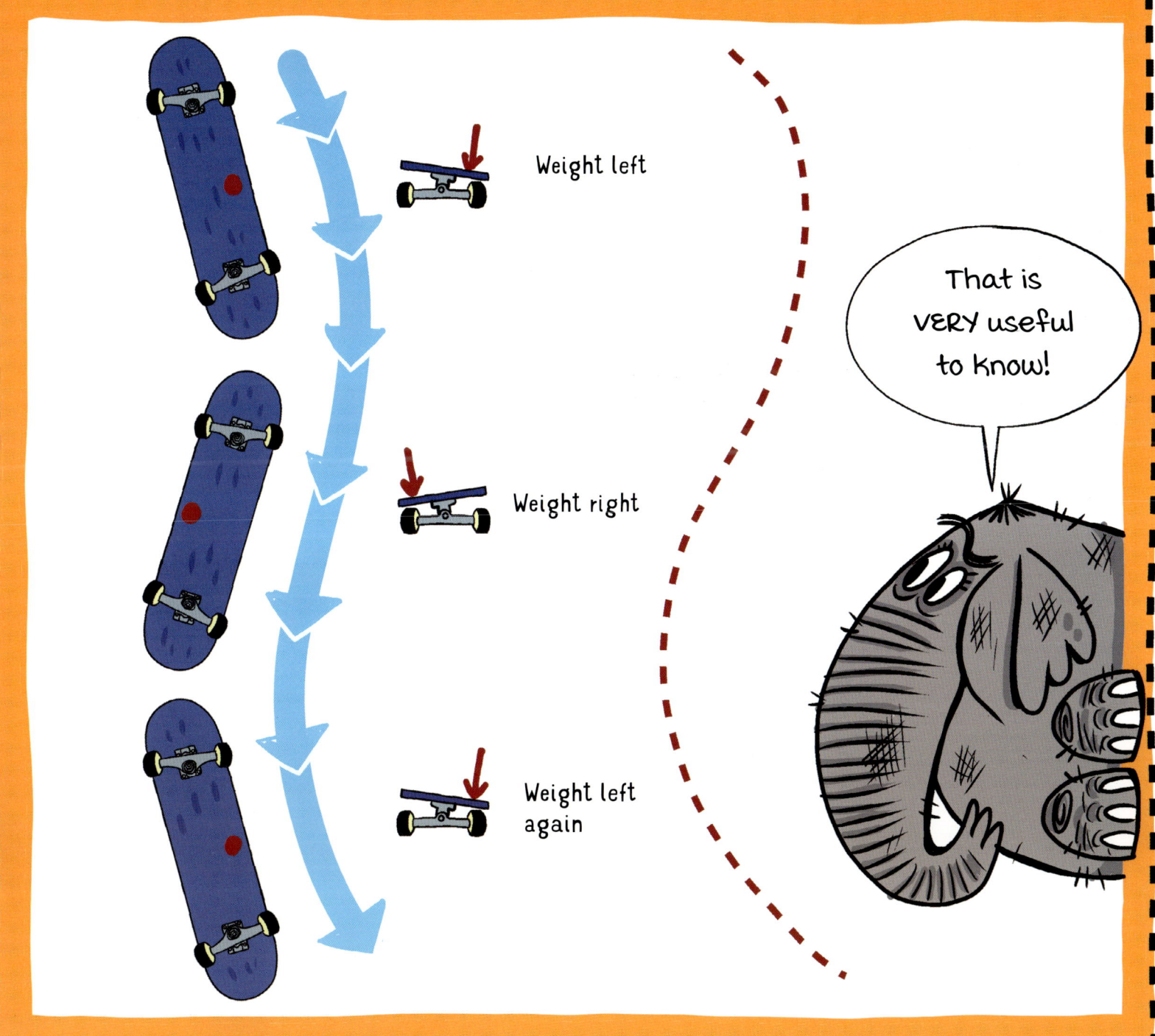

SLALOM SKILLS

Now you know how to turn the skateboard, it's time for some slalom practice.

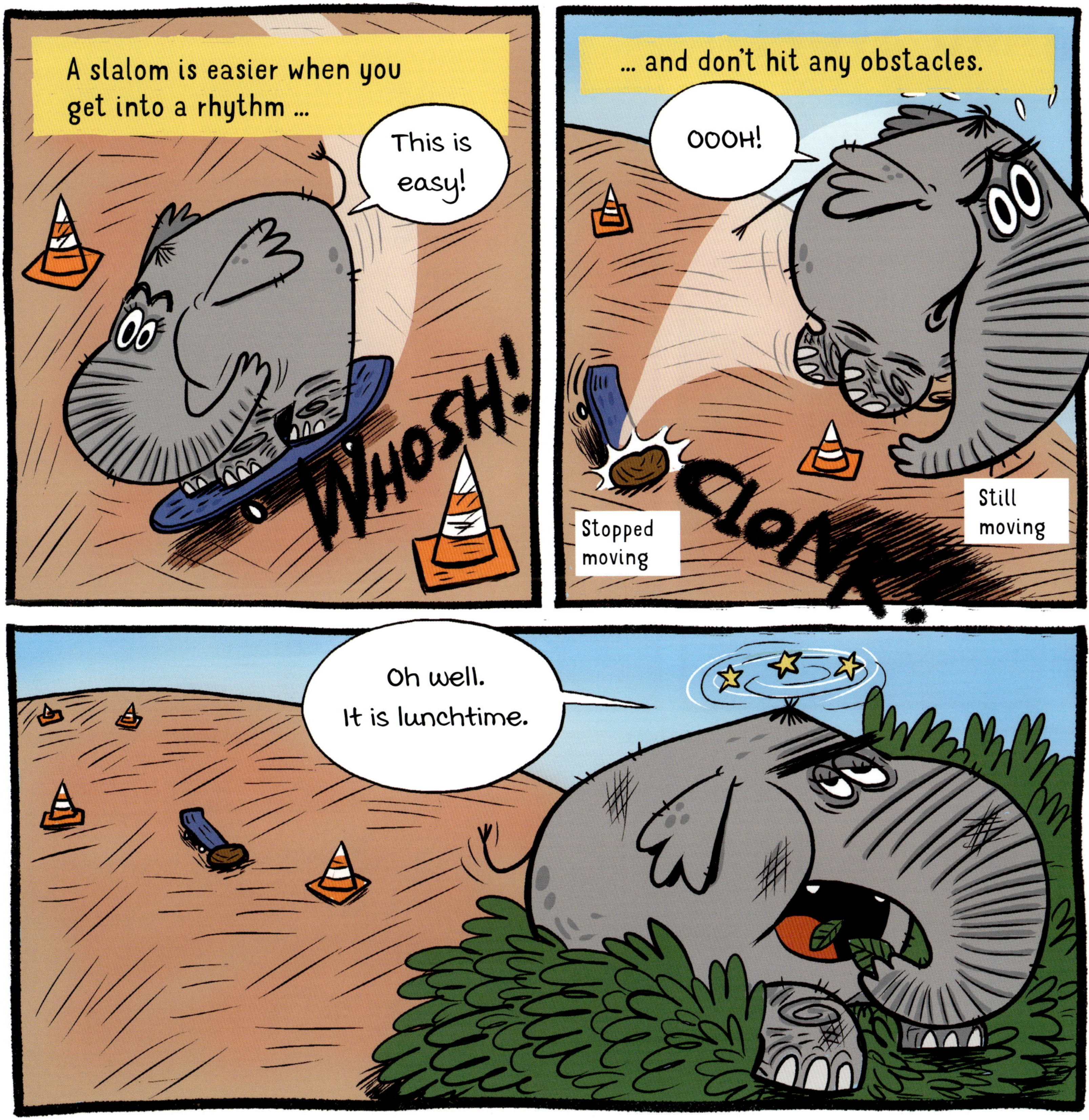

HARD STOP!

Once moving, objects keep moving in a straight line – unless a force affects them.

Like when I was learning. Friction pulled me back.

Exactly. Friction slowed the wheels down.

But the rock didn't slow me down ...

No! The rock was too big to roll over. When the wheels hit it, the rock didn't move – it pushed back. The skateboard stopped moving.

Coming through!

No you're not.

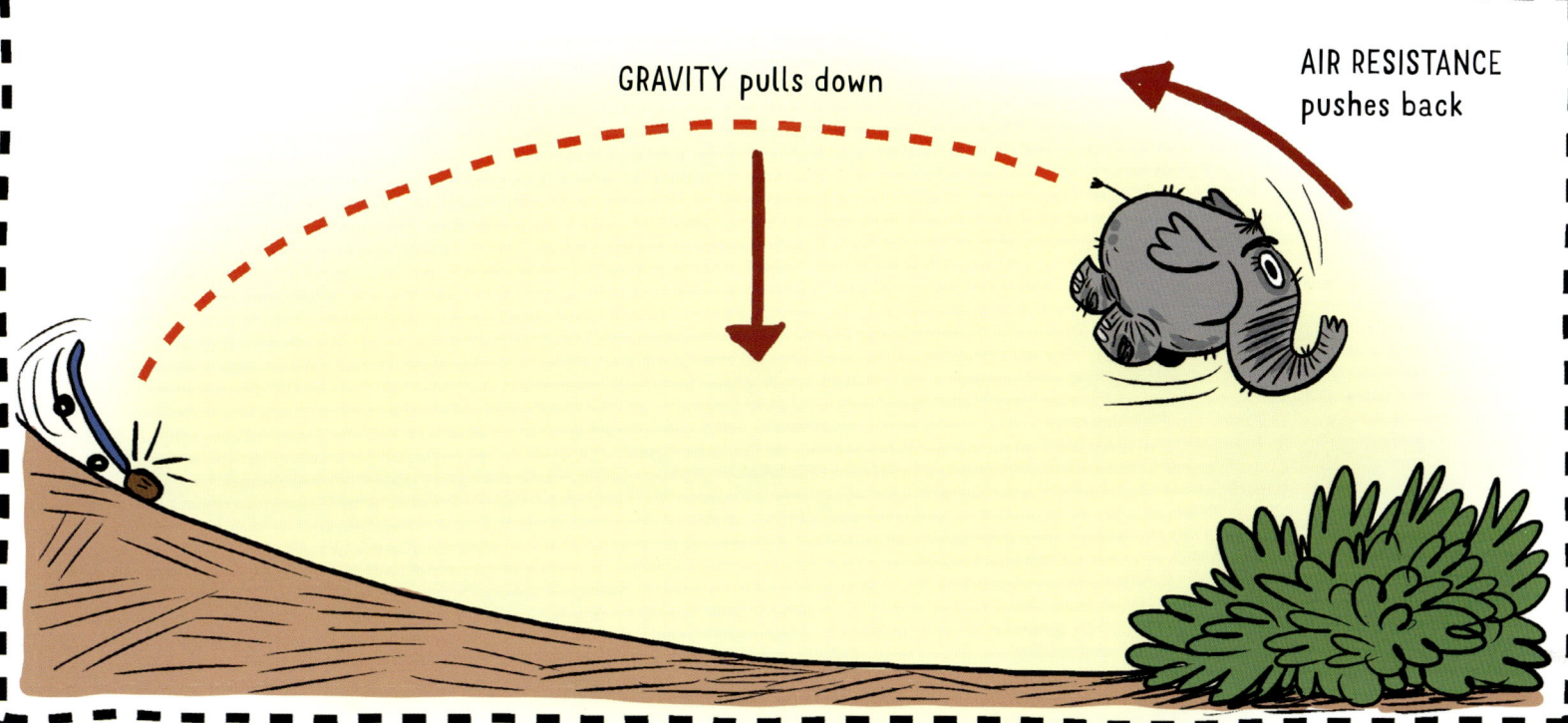

AT THE SKATE PARK

Once you can skateboard along and do turns, it's time for a new challenge.

SPEED THIEF (PART 2)

The skateboard went slower and slower on the ramp because friction and gravity BOTH stole its speed.

The skateboard was moving fastest after the push-off.

PUSH
MOTION

Friction slowed it down...

MOTION
Friction of wheels and ground
Friction of moving parts inside wheel

... and so did air resistance.

FLAP! FLAP!
MOTION
AIR RESISTANCE

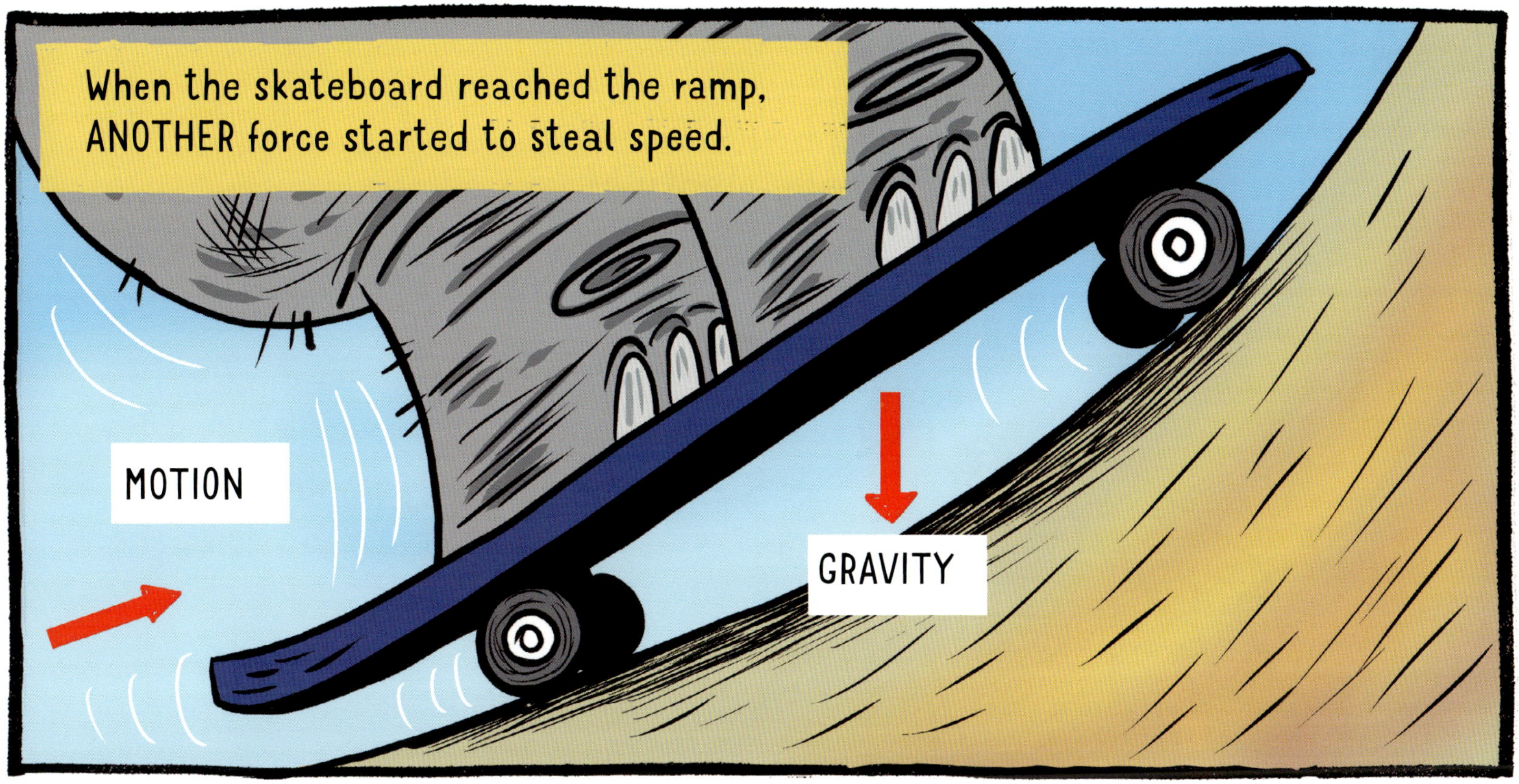

When the skateboard reached the ramp, ANOTHER force started to steal speed.

MOTION

GRAVITY

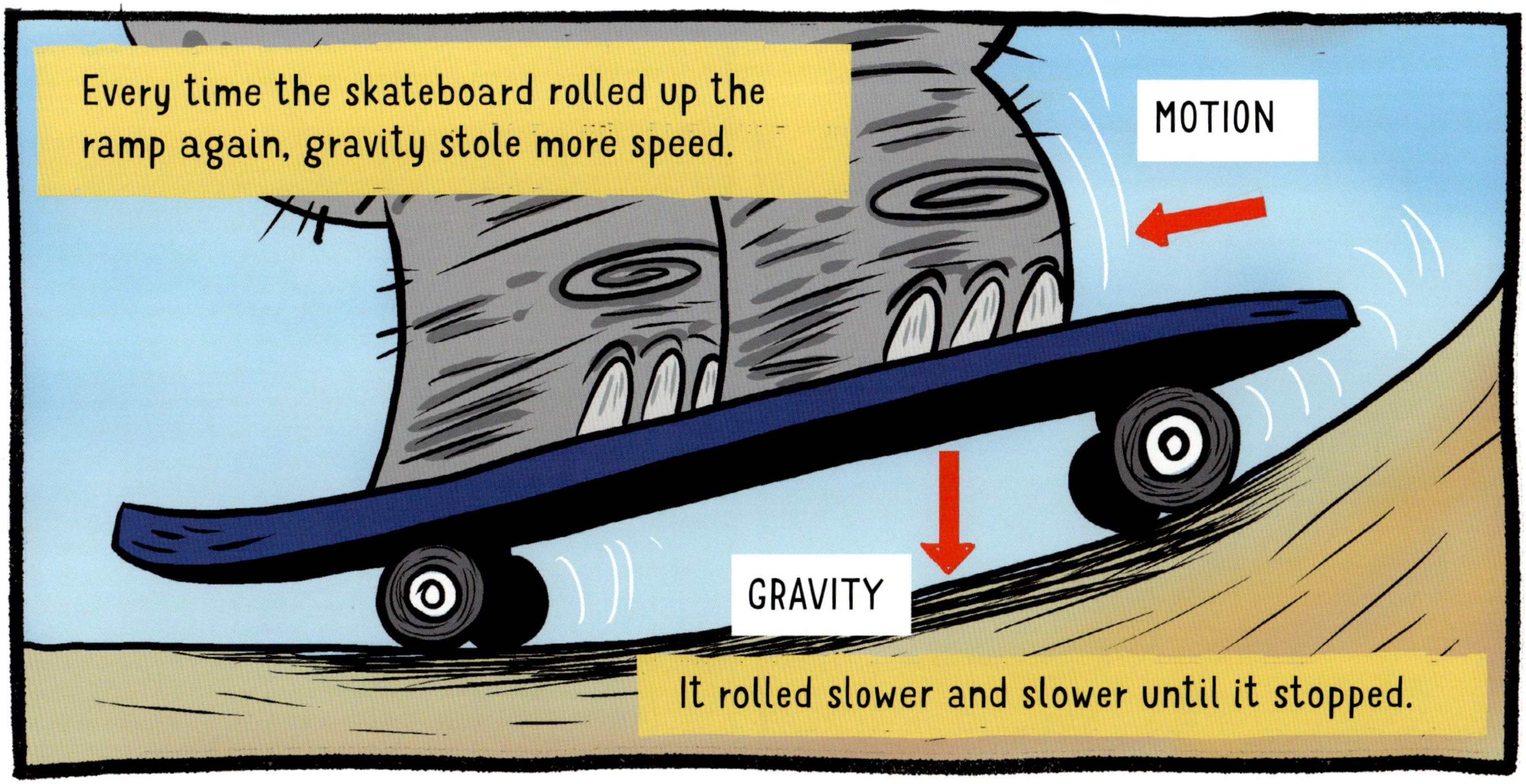

Every time the skateboard rolled up the ramp again, gravity stole more speed.

MOTION

GRAVITY

It rolled slower and slower until it stopped.

FASTER, FASTER!

Where can the skateboard get MORE speed? Well – from something most elephants have plenty of ...

SKATE SCHOOL FOR ELEPHANTS?

So, do you REALLY still want to become a skate teacher?

"Hmm. Good question."

"I'd need to get the learners moving."

"You need a push to move."

"Impossible."

"How do you stand on THAT?"

"No way."

PAF!

They learnt friction and gravity slows them down.

"I've slowed down."

"Well I've stopped."

"Woo-ahh! Backward!"

BONUS ELEPHANT FACTS

1. They're BIG! African elephants are the world's biggest land animal. Even a baby weighs about 120 kg. Grown-ups weigh over 6 tonnes.

2. Their trunks are amazing. An elephant's trunk is much more sensitive than a fingertip. It contains thousands of muscles and can hold 8 litres of water.

3. They're always eating! When you're that big, you need a lot of food: up to 150 kg per day. Elephants also drink over 100 litres of water a day.

4. They poo ... a lot! What goes in eventually has to come out. Adult elephants release over 90 kg of poo a day. They also fart a lot.

5. Baby elephants can walk within an hour of being born, and keep up with the herd after two days. They cannot actually skateboard, though.

6. Elephants can't jump. In fact, elephants are the only land mammal that can't. They're just not built for it.

7. Elephants hardly sleep. In the wild, African elephants sleep about two hours per day. (Imagine how grumpy you'd be on two hours' sleep!)

GLOSSARY

accelerate move more quickly (for example, when you pedal harder on a bicycle it accelerates, or goes faster)

air invisible combination of gases surrounding Earth, which living things need to survive

air resistance also called 'drag', a frictional force that happens when something moves though air

airs short for 'aerial trick' – term used in skateboarding to perfom a trick where all four wheels leave the ground

friction pulling or slowing-down force between two things moving past each other while touching (for example, a scooter's brake touching the wheel, slowing the scooter down)

gas material that can change its shape and size to fit its container

liquid material that can change its shape to fit a container, but not its size

slalom a downhill course often marked by poles, flags or cones

solid material that does not change its shape or size unless forced to do so

speed how far you travel in a set time (for example, 70 km in one hour). A longer distance means a higher speed

troupe group or band, especially of travelling entertainers

water resistance frictional force that happens when something moves through water

INDEX

accelerate 26, 29, 31

air resistance 13, 21, 24, 31

airs 5, 31

balance 8

deck 7, 8, 10

friction 12, 20, 24, 28, 31

gas 13
gravity 21, 25, 28

liquid 13

motion 9, 10, 24-25

object 13

pull 16
push 9 16

skate park 4, 22-23
slaom 18-19
speed 26

ramp 22

troupe 4, 31
trucks 16

weight 8, 10, 17, 29

wheels 16, 20, 24

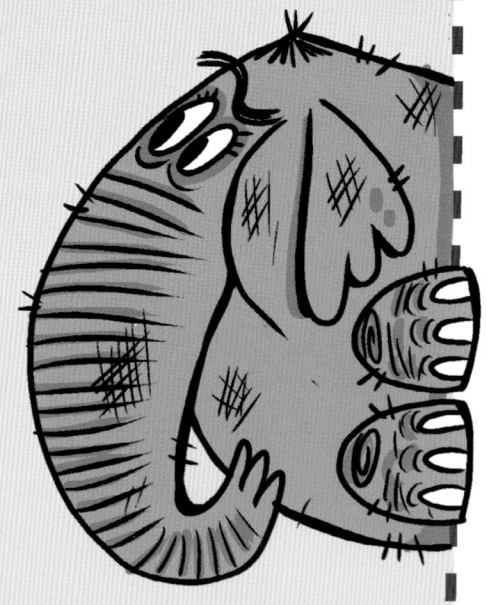